BRITANNICA BEGINNINGS

MO WILLEMS
AWARD-WINNING CHILDREN'S AUTHOR AND ANIMATOR

PAULA MORROW

Britannica®
Educational Publishing

IN ASSOCIATION WITH

ROSEN
EDUCATIONAL SERVICES

Published in 2015 by Britannica Educational Publishing (a trademark of Encyclopædia Britannica, Inc.) in association with The Rosen Publishing Group, Inc.
29 East 21st Street, New York, NY 10010

Distributed exclusively by Rosen Publishing.
To see additional Britannica Educational Publishing titles, go to rosenpublishing.com.

First Edition

Britannica Educational Publishing
J.E. Luebering: Director, Core Reference Group
Mary Rose McCudden: Editor, Britannica Student Encyclopedia

Rosen Publishing
Hope Lourie Killcoyne: Executive Editor
Shalini Saxena: Editor
Nelson Sá: Art Director
Michael Moy: Designer
Cindy Reiman: Photography Manager

Library of Congress Cataloging-in-Publication Data

Morrow, Paula, author.
Mo Willems/Paula Morrow.—First Edition.
          pages cm.—(Britannica beginner bios)
Includes bibliographical references and index.
ISBN 978-1-62275-685-8 (library bound) — ISBN 978-1-62275-686-5 (pbk.) —
ISBN 978-1-62275-687-2 (6-pack)
1. Willems, Mo—Juvenile literature. 2. Illustrators—United States—Biography—Juvenile literature. I. Title.
NC975.5.W519M67 2014
741.6'42092—dc23

Manufactured in the United States of America

CONTENTS

CHAPTER ONE

PASSION AND PERSISTENCE

Mo Willems is the creator of many successful children's books. He is the mind behind such popular characters as the Pigeon, Knuffle Bunny, and Elephant and Piggie. He is a gifted artist and

Mo Willems enjoys reading his books out loud. This book is *Leonardo the Terrible Monster.*

4

a funny person. However, Willems needed other qualities to have such well-loved characters make the leap

from his imagination to a finished book. He had passion. He had PERSISTENCE.

Willems had always loved drawing. He really wanted to write words to go with his

Doodling helps an artist develop ideas. Sometimes it takes lots of doodles to figure out what a picture will be.

pictures. He was passionate about making a picture book. Willems tried for many years. He was persistent about making his dream come true.

Then one day his **AGENT** saw Willems's sketches of a pigeon. She

The Pigeon is the star of Mo Willems's first book. Now there are several books about the Pigeon.

Vocabulary Box

An **AGENT** is someone who helps writers find a publisher to produce their books.

liked them and asked him to turn them into a book. Those sketches became *Don't Let the Pigeon Drive the Bus!* That was the first of Willems's many books.

Quick Fact

The Caldecott Medal is given every year to the best new picture book. A few books are named Caldecott Honor Books. *Don't Let the Pigeon Drive the Bus!* was a Caldecott Honor Book in 2004.

CHAPTER TWO

EARLY LIFE

Mo Willems was born on February 11, 1968, in Des Plaines, Illinois. His parents had moved there from the Netherlands. A few years later, the family moved to New Orleans, Louisiana. Willems grew up there and thinks of it as his hometown.

As a boy, Willems loved cartoons and comics. His favorite comic strip was *Peanuts.* Young Mo doodled and drew

Charles M. Schulz drew the *Peanuts* comic strip, which Willems loved as a child. Here are Snoopy, Lucy, Charlie Brown, and Linus.

all the time. He copied Charlie Brown and Snoopy. He dreamed of drawing his own comic strip when he grew up.

In high school, Willems drew comic strips for his school newspaper. He also liked to act in school plays. He put together his passion for cartooning and his passion for acting. Willems became a stand-up comedian. He wrote jokes to tell an audience.

After he finished high school,

A stand-up comedian can make people laugh by using only his voice and his actions to tell stories and jokes.

9

Animators use different tools. Some animators use ink and paint. Others use computers. Some even use clay.

Willems went to London, England. He spent the summer there doing stand-up comedy. He learned what people thought was funny. Willems then went to college at New York University. There he studied filmmaking. He soon

Vocabulary Box

ANIMATION is the process of making pictures that seem to move. Animated movies are made up of many separate drawings. Each drawing is a little different than the one before. When the drawings are quickly shown in order, one after another, the figures seem to move.

Traveling alone let Willems see the world. Everywhere he went, he drew the things he saw.

realized that he wanted to focus on **ANIMATION**.

When Willems finished college, he did not get a job right away. For a whole year he traveled by himself. He visited faraway places. He met all kinds of people. He

11

Quick Fact

The first comic character Mo Willems drew was a space hero named Lazer Brain. Lazer Brain was not really a hero. Whatever he did, he just made things worse.

visited 30 countries. Every day he sketched or doodled in his notebook. That notebook was published in 2006 as *You Can Never Find a Rickshaw When It Monsoons: The World on One Cartoon a Day.*

CHAPTER THREE

EARLY CAREER

In 1993, Willems moved to Brooklyn, New York. He continued to make movies, doodle, and sketch. He sold some of his cartoons to magazines. That year he made his first cartoon book. First he made some sketches. Then he took the pieces of paper with

The Brooklyn Bridge connects Brooklyn, where Willems lived, with Manhattan, where he worked.

his sketches and stapled them together to make his own book. He gave copies to his friends and family.

People liked his sketchbook. After that, Willems made a new sketchbook every year. They were fun to make. He could try out new ideas. He felt free to be creative and not worry about making mistakes.

Sketching captures shapes and moods. Later, the artist can make a more detailed drawing from the sketch.

In 1994, Willems got a job writing for the television show *Sesame Street*. He was hired because he was funny. Part of his job was writing the things that the character Elmo said. He also made short animated movies for the show.

Willems said working at *Sesame Street* taught him to "write funny." Muppets like Elmo (wearing a suit here) helped make his words even funnier.

One of the characters in some of his short movies was Suzie Kabloozie. He worked at *Sesame Street* for nine years.

Willems also wrote other cartoon television shows. One of those was *Sheep in the Big City*.

Quick Fact

Mo Willems won six Emmy Awards in nine years at *Sesame Street*. Emmy Awards are given each year for the work that people do on television shows.

After a while Willems wanted to try to write children's picture books. So he took time off from his job and worked on ideas for books. He also doodled. The books were not very good, but the doodles were fun. One doodle was a pigeon. That pigeon

When Willems talks to groups of children, he shows them how he draws the pictures in his books. The Pigeon started out as a doodle.

started in the margin of a notebook. Willems said it complained that it was better than the other doodles and wanted to star in a book.

Willems had to go back to his job. He wrote more scripts for television. But just for fun, he turned his pigeon doodles into a sketchbook. His agent liked his silly pigeon. She asked him to put the pigeon into a picture book. The book became *Don't Let the Pigeon Drive the Bus!* It changed Willems's life.

CHAPTER FOUR

MASTER OF THE DOODLE

People loved *Don't Let the Pigeon Drive the Bus!* The book won many awards. Readers wanted more books by Mo Willems. He has made more than 50 books already. And he is still writing.

The Pigeon gets very upset about wanting to drive the bus. Willems always reads this book in a loud, lively voice.

Don't Let the Pigeon Drive the Bus! is about a pigeon who wants to drive a bus. The bus driver tells the readers not to let the pigeon take over, but the pigeon keeps asking if it can drive the bus. Readers like to keep telling the bird "No!" This book is different from other picture books. The pictures look like doodles, but they show real feelings. The pigeon is sad and angry and cute and funny. Readers become part of the story as they read.

Willems's second book was *Knuffle Bunny*. A little girl named Trixie

The Pigeon became famous in other countries, too. Here, it is in Scotland talking to a small audience.

19

loses her toy bunny. She cannot talk yet, so she cannot tell her father what is wrong. The story is based on something that happened to Willems's own daughter. Her name is also Trixie. Willems took photographs for this book. Then he drew his cartoons on the photos. It looks like the cartoon people are in a real city.

Willems's next challenge was to write books for beginning readers. The result was the Elephant and Piggie series. There are more than 20 books in the series. Elephant and Piggie are very different from each other. Elephant is often sad and quiet. Piggie is loud

Children love the Elephant and Piggie books. These books are easy to read. They are also very funny.

Quick Fact

The Theodor Seuss Geisel Medal is given every year to the best book for beginning readers. Elephant and Piggie books have won two medals as well as several other honors.

and happy. But they are good friends. Willems thinks the Elephant and Piggie books work well if two people read the books together. An adult can read what Elephant says. A child can read what Piggie says.

Willems also writes plays. Some are based on his books. His first play was about Knuffle Bunny. In the play, Trixie cannot talk, just like in the book. So her songs in the play have no words. She sings silly sounds. Later, Willems wrote *Elephant & Piggie's We Are in a Play!*

Children can also access Willems's creations through two **APPS**. One is Don't Let the

Vocabulary Box

An **APP** is a game that can be played on a tablet or a smartphone.

21

Willems explains how to use his new app. The pictures on the board show what the app can do.

Pigeon Run This App! Another is Mo . . . On the Go! The apps let children dance, draw, and even drive the bus.

Some of Willems's art is in museums. The Eric Carle Museum of Picture Book Art in Amherst,

The Eric Carle Museum of Picture Book Art shows art from many famous books and authors. It even has a giant red elephant sculpture that Willems made.

Massachusetts, had a whole show of Willems's art. Eric Carle, the author of *The Very Hungry Caterpillar*, said Willems is "a master of the doodle, sketch, cartoon, and scribble."

CHAPTER FIVE

SHARING HIS DREAM

At the Willems house, the whole family doodles. The dining room walls are chalkboard, and the table has a big paper cover. After dinner, Willems doodles. His wife and his daughter doodle. If they have guests, the guests doodle, too.

Willems wants children to draw their own pictures. He wants them to write their own books. His books

Willems loves to see children draw and make up their own stories. He says everyone should doodle every day.

are a good place to start. Children can copy the Pigeon, just as Willems copied Charlie Brown and Snoopy. They can make new stories about the Pigeon. Then they can create their own characters.

Willems has a lot of ideas for new books. When he is making a book, he reads the words. He looks at the

Willems enjoys visiting schools to read his books. He likes to talk with children and hear what they think.

pictures. If the words make sense with no pictures, there are too many words. If the pictures make sense without the words, there are too many pictures. The words and the pictures have to need each other.

Willems even used a radio show to encourage people to think about words and pictures. Radio does not seem like a good way for a cartoonist to show his art, but Willems made it work. He described a picture. He also had a copy of the picture on a website. He asked his listeners to tell him what they thought the caption should say. They could call the radio station or write the caption on the website. Then he told them his own idea for a caption.

Quick Fact

Mo Willems wants children to add their ideas to his books. He says he writes 49 percent of a book. He wants his readers to put in the other 51 percent.

On the wall is a portrait Willems drew of himself. He continues to make a new doodle or sketch every day.

It takes lots of practice to be a writer. It takes lots of practice to be an artist. Everything you draw gives you more practice. Willems thinks, "There is no such thing as a 'wrong' drawing."

Willems says he does not *write* books. He *makes* them. He says he is not an artist. He is a **CRAFTSMAN**. An artist wants to make his audience understand him. A craftsman wants to understand his audience.

Vocabulary Box

A CRAFTSMAN is a skilled worker who makes things, often by hand.

27

TIMELINE

1968: Willems is born on February 11 in Des Plaines, Illinois.

1972: The Willems family moves to New Orleans, Louisiana.

1990: Willems graduates from New York University's Tisch School of the Arts.

1993: Willems moves to Brooklyn, New York.

1994: Willems is hired as a regular writer for *Sesame Street*.

1997: Willems marries Cheryl Camp in Brooklyn.

2003: Willems publishes *Don't Let the Pigeon Drive the Bus!* It is named a Caldecott Honor Book.

2004: *Knuffle Bunny: A Cautionary Tale* is published. It is named a Caldecott Honor Book.

2006: *You Can Never Find a Rickshaw When It Monsoons: The World on One Cartoon a Day* is published.

2006: *Edwina, the Dinosaur Who Didn't Know She Was Extinct* is published.

2007: *Knuffle Bunny Too: A Case of Mistaken Identity* is published. It is named a Caldecott Honor Book.

2007: The first Elephant and Piggie books are published.

2008: Willems moves from New York to Northampton, Massachusetts.

2009: *Big Frog Can't Fit In: A Pop Out Book* is published.

2009: *Naked Mole Rat Gets Dressed* is published.

TIMELINE

2011: Willems creates the app Don't Let the Pigeon Run This App!

2012: *Goldilocks and the Three Dinosaurs: As Retold by Mo Willems* is published.

2012: *The Duckling Gets a Cookie?!* is published.

2013: *Don't Pigeonhole Me! Two Decades of the Mo Willems Sketchbook* is published.

2013: Willems leaves the United States to live in Paris for a year. He sketches daily.

2014: *The Pigeon Needs a Bath* is published.

2014: *A Big Guy Took My Ball!* is named a Theodor Seuss Geisel Honor Book.

GLOSSARY

AUDIENCE A group of people who gather to listen to or watch something.

COMEDIAN A person who tells jokes to make people laugh.

COMPLAIN To grumble, fuss, or whine.

DOODLE A silly drawing; to doodle is to scribble or draw.

KNUFFLE Pronounced "kuh – NUF – ful"; a hug or cuddle.

MARGIN The empty part at the edges of a page.

MUSEUM A place where things of lasting value are kept.

PASSION A very strong feeling or feelings.

PUBLISHER A person or company that prints and sells books, magazines, newspapers, or other materials.

REJECT To say no to; turn down.

SCRIPT The words that actors say in a play, a movie, or a television show.

FOR MORE INFORMATION

BOOKS

Colich, Abby. *Mo Willems*. North Mankato, MN: Capstone Press, 2014.

Llanas, Sheila Griffin. *Mo Willems*. Minneapolis, MN: ABDO Publishing, 2012.

Willems, Mo. *Don't Pigeonhole Me! Two Decades of the Mo Willems Sketchbook*. New York, NY: Disney Books, 2013.

Willems, Mo. *You Can Never Find a Rickshaw When It Monsoons: The World on One Cartoon a Day*. New York, NY: Hyperion, 2006.

WEBSITES

Because of the changing nature of Internet links, Rosen Publishing has developed an online list of websites related to the subject of this book. This site is updated regularly. Please use this link to access the list:

http://www.rosenlinks.com/BBB/Will

INDEX